WAYS OF LOVING

LOVING

JOHN C.
EDWARDS

S.J.

SEX

CHASTITY

THE MASS

By the same author:
Ways of Praying
Ways of Forgiveness

Imprimatur:
Very Rev Canon Frank Diamond
Diocesan Administrator
Northampton (Sede vacante)
30th August 1989

ISBN 1 871217 04 0

Published by
Family Publications
Wicken, Milton Keynes, MK19 6BU
Telephone: 0908 57234

Cover design by the
Benedictine Sisters at Turvey Abbey

Printed in Great Britain by
BPCC Wheatons Ltd
Marsh Barton, Exeter, EX2 8RP

Fr John C Edwards, SJ was born in Sussex in 1929. He entered the Royal Naval College, Dartmouth at the age of 13, went to sea in 1947 and served in the Korean war. He left the Navy in 1953 to seek his vocation, undertaking studies, noviceship and formation in the Society of Jesus until 1968, the last two years of which were spent in Rome. He was ordained Priest in 1964, and since 1968 has served three years in parishes, and the remainder in retreat work and parish missions which have taken him to the USA, Mauritius and various countries in Africa.

Contents:

Six: Do I really think God is lovable?

Appendices:

Foreword

"What is love?" "How do we love?" After the Sexual Revolution, many people are asking these basic questions. They want to go beyond the biological experience of sexuality. Some of them have been wounded by a selfish quest for pleasure, or betrayed by relationships distorted by a false understanding of "love". They want to know whether there is a better way. They are looking for the source of love and the meaning of love.

At the same time, young people in particular are entitled to wise guidance in a society where the effects of the Sexual Revolution are all around us. Should they not be spared the mistakes and sorrows of the previous generations? They too are asking questions about love and they deserve true and honest answers, not the commercialised emotionalism of the pop culture, not the lies of "value free" sexologists.

In response to this search for the truth of love, Fr John Edwards S J provides his own blueprint or guide to the divine art of loving. However, if some readers are surprised at the sub-title of this book, "Sex, Chastity, The Mass", they should remember that a Catholic blueprint for love brings together the human and the divine. Catholicism is the religion of the Incarnation. Our God took our flesh in the Person of Jesus Christ. He lived, died and rose again in that human flesh. He showed us that our bodies are meant to be temples of his Holy Spirit. He raised sexuality, in marriage, to be a sacrament of his sacrificial love. In the Eucharist he gives us his Body for our bodies. Through the sacraments he guides us into the true ways of loving.

1

Therefore, I warmly welcome and commend this wise priest's blueprint for love. May the readers of this book take it to heart and so be led closer to Him whose undying love shows us how to love one another.

Edouard Cardinal Gagnon, PSS
President
Pontifical Council for the Family
Vatican City State
August 1989

One:

Preliminary

1. What this book is about

Love is the most important thing in the world, and we are made for it. But this book obviously leaves enormous gaps in dealing with ways of loving — and in types of loving.

It touches only on a few aspects of some of the more important or more controverted or more neglected ways of loving. It is a partial blue-print. For whom? In the part on sex and marriage I envisage thinking teenagers as my readers. In the rest, I envisage, as well as them, ''Religious'' and thinking Christians generally. My belief is that one cannot see how wonderful chastity is unless you first understand how wonderful sex is.

2. What is love?

We can agree that in all loving worthy of the name there must be one essential element. Whatever the type of love or style of loving or purity of devotion or heat of emotion or tenaciousness of fidelity, this must be present: *the good of the beloved.* Nothing can be given the name of love, let us agree, if it militates against the other person's good, whether the other person be man, or God himself.

Of course, it is a minimum definition that love should be ''to want and to intend the good of the other person''. But it still brings with it immense implications. First, if I am to love properly, I must know what is ''good'' for the other person: I must know therefore what he is *for*: I must know

God's will and mind about the other person and about the relationship. Secondly, love is not primarily a matter of feeling. If it were, God could never *order* me to love. He does: he tells me to love my enemies; but if love were essentially a matter of feelings, God would be ordering me to change my feelings, which usually cannot be done. Further, no one could ever marry. For in marriage you promise to love. But you can only promise what is in your control. No man can promise to preserve his feelings indefinitely into the future: he knows that at eighty he will not feel exactly as he does for his bride when they marry in their twenties. What he is promising is something over and above his feelings; he promises what is in his control or what he can effect.

Moreover love is often at its highest and clearest in opposition to feelings: could we deny the name of "love" to the faithful performance of duty — to the fireman, say, who enters the blaze certainly not with joy; with pity perhaps, but mainly because it is his duty?

Did Jesus in Gethsemane act as he did because he was emotionally attracted to his Father's will?

That said, ideally there *should* be feeling. To "want what is the best for the other person" means to want humanly. There should if possible be more than the cold act of the will, the simple decision to choose well. There should be a total wanting — with will of course, but heart (nerves, blood, emotions) too. That is what simple people mean by love, and it's what very spiritual people may forget (especially if they are intellectuals and, dare we say, anglo-saxons as well). In religion, it leads to the blight that ridicules a spirituality using sacramentals as being primitive, and devotion to the Sacred Heart as being emotional.

3. Love in a Christian

No Christian should ever think of love without remembering

what it means to belong to Christ. The Christian in a "state of grace" is lived in by Christ. From God's point of view the Christian is just one of the ways in which His Son is able to extend the effect of His Incarnation. It is Jesus who, now at this moment, wants to serve and love these people through me. Thus every part of me, every movement of will, every involvement of blood or nerve, every impulse of emotion, should ideally be conformed to Christ, and should be an apt vehicle for his love; should be as nearly as what they would be for him if he were in my place. Anything less (and of course it always will be less) is a frustration of the loving-power of Jesus, which he intends to exercise now through me, if I would let him.

Most clearly of all is this seen in forgiveness of enemies. *Of course* Jesus will order us to love our enemies; isn't this his own typical, essential work? Since he gave himself, and his life, to those who crucified him, is it strange that (united with him and claiming to have the same mind and heart as he), he should expect us to live the same way? Part of the reason for him having united with him is that we should allow him to live in us the way he wants.

4. Background

The most intelligible book I know about love is C S Lewis' *The Four Loves*. Fr Thomas Dubay S.M. seems to me the master on Religious Life: *" . . . And you are Christ's"* is the most relevant book on our topic; its subtitle is *The charism of virginity and the Celibate life.* Both these books have guided me.

The New Testament is quoted from the Knox Version. Church Documents are taken from Flannery, *Vatican II*, volumes 1 & 2. Italics in citations are my own. A good deal of New Testament and Church Documents are quoted. It is not pretended that you can prove things from texts: but you can adduce the mind of Christ and his Church on some points.

Details of these books and other recommmended reading are given in Appendix 3.

Ways of Loving is meant to fit in with *Ways of Praying* and *Ways of Forgiveness* (the latter being on the Sacrament of Reconciliation). I am deeply grateful to Denis Riches of *Family Publications* for producing them.

Any good points in this booklet are due to my family and my brothers in the Society of Jesus, especially Fr Thomas Conlan. Also in various ways to Dr Karen Groves, John Kelly FRCS, Monica Knight, Peter McDonald, Valerie and Denis Riches. And to the following religious sisters: Anne-Marie Farasyn, Monica Gribbin, and Nuala O'Connor.

An apology: reams of theology (especially moral theology) are dismissed in silence; controverted positions are blandly over-simplified; pain-points which cry out for compassionate treatment are ignored; mystical depths go unplumbed or are blithely jumped across. This is not just because of limitations in the author: the obvious fact is that this sort of book about love, for the sort of people likely to read it, can't go on for ever. Better *something* should be said than nothing; if a thing is worth doing it's worth doing badly. Better to risk looking a fool when you're trying to help, than not to try to help at all.

And it is certain the teenagers and Religious do need help . . .

John C Edwards, S J
Farm Street, London
August 1989

Two:

Sex and Marriage

1. The "Three Links" of sex

If one wants to know what a thing is for — something very precious and very beautiful — one goes to the experts. Sex is precious and beautiful. But who are the experts? I would say: not the psychiatrists, not the marriage counsellors — and not even the priests. The experts in sex are lovers.

But they must be real lovers. That is (again) they must want the best for *the other*. They must therefore be unselfish people. They need not be old, but they must be 'mature'. And, so that it should be quite clear, let us say that these two good lovers have sex, completely, for the first time. Let these be our experts.

If such a couple could put into words what they experience, we would learn something about sex. Imagine therefore as honestly as possible what these two generous young lovers might say — supposing they were to speak. First the girl. (She really loves, remember, and it is her first experience).

"For this to be true and complete, I must know that you understand what it means to me. Because of what we have done, I am now a different person. Not just in my body (that is really the least of it) but in my very self. It is not just my body which I gave to you and which has been changed, it is my very self. It is *I*, totally, who have been "possessed" by you. And I see now why they use that word: I can never be the same again now. And I want you to know that I am very, very glad. Glad to have been possessed by you; glad to have given myself to you; very, very glad that it is *you* who have changed me.''

Something like that, surely? And the last sentence? If she was not in fact glad, would we not feel pity? (''Poor child — what was wrong? She should be *happy* about it'').

And the man: what would he want to say; he who also is, remember, a good lover? Surely it would be something like this:

''Please do not think that for me this has just been an experience of pleasure. It is not just my seed I have given you, drawn from my body by conditioned reflex — a sort of automatic tribute paid from my body to your beauty. It is that of course, but there is far more. It is not simply my seed I give you, it is my self. And there is nothing automatic in the gift — it is free and deliberate. It really is my *life* I give you, and in any sense you care to name I would indeed 'give my life' for you. And know this: I am abashed, humbled, amazed, exalted that you should allow me to give my life to you, allow me to promise you my self. And it *is* a promise: never to any other woman could I say this, or 'say' it in this way''.

Too chivalrous, too purple? At least some of my readers will recognise that this fits reality not just as they would like it to be, but as they know it is.

Now all this has been written without mention of God. Or of babies. I have simply said ''Listen to their heart-beats''. But now let us bring God into it, or at least the Church. What does the Church (old Mother Church) say? She leans over the young lovers, taps them both on the shoulders, and says:

''Exactly! Quite right, my dears. You understand exactly. You my dear gave yourself, completely, to him, and were glad to. And you, yes you were privileged to give your life and self to her. That's exactly what I say! All I ask'', says the Church (here turning to the man) ''is that before

8

saying this with your bodies, as you so properly and so beautifully have, you should have first stood up with her at your side, before witnesses, (and preferably with her Mum and Dad within earshot) and said out loud with your lips — calling Almighty God to witness — what you have just stated with your bodies. And then sign a legal document to say you've said it. In short, get married first''.

Plainly that is not an obligation laid on extrinsically by a group of elderly clerical bachelors in Rome: it comes from the very nature of sexual intercourse, rightly understood. The act of sex itself, our ''experts'' would say, tells us in heart, nerves, and blood that it involves a complete gift of self. That means a total, exclusive and permanent gift. If you don't see this, Christians would say, your heart (if not your nerves and blood) needs refining: and you don't know much about sex. Expressed succinctly and negatively, all this adds up to ''Outside of marriage, no sexual intercourse''. Or ''Sexual intercourse is meant to go with marriage''.

We have therefore two links of a chain. The first, sexual intercourse, is linked to a second: life-long, total, permanent commitment.

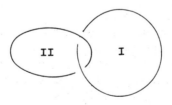

But there is a preceding link. Before intercourse can occur, there has to be something else. There has to be the arousal of passion. Physically, this must happen: no arousal (to be specific, erection in the man), no intercourse. The two things are linked; indeed arousal is clamouring to be completed —

not surprisingly, that is the biological purpose of arousal, that is what the whole process is "for". Sexual passion is linked psychologically and biologically to intercourse.

And so there is a third link:

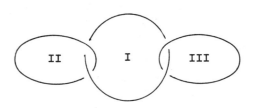

Here comes therefore the news that sounds so bad to modern ears. If I is linked to II, and III is linked to I — then III is linked to II. I was intercourse, II was marriage, III was arousal of passion. So we get the hard saying **"Outside of Marriage no deliberate** *(Deliberate: intended)* **— no deliberate, willed, intended experience of sexual pleasure at all"**.

Does the Church really say that? More to the point, does God?

2. Our Lord's words and meaning

As it happens, Mt 5:28 is quite explicit. "I tell you that he who casts his eyes on a woman so as to lust after her has already committed adultery with her in his heart". I do not know exactly what our Lord means, but this much is obvious: the man who goes to a strip club, the boy who buys a pornographic magazine, the masturbator, could be (*could be* — it is *not impossible* that such a person *could be*) committing sin which *could be* very serious.

Of course the statement is shorthand. To make it more tolerable let us spell out what the Church, what Jesus, *what God* is saying. Can it be, to the girl, anything less than this?

"Look: not just before you lie with a man, before you give yourself to him completely, before he takes complete possession of you, are you to hear him promise out loud before witnesses — and before Me — that he will give his life for you. Not merely is the complete possession of you something so wonderful and so beautiful that before a man is entitled to it he must promise you his life. Not just before he lies with you . . . but before he touches you, caresses you in certain ways — even before he kisses you in certain ways . . . for even that much constitutes a claim, even a possession, so great that before he is entitled to it he must promise you his life. And know that *that* is the value of your beauty and of your womanhood".

Say that is hard, and I totally agree. Tell me few people see it and even fewer try to live up to it, and I agree. Tell me it is impossible, and I say you're wrong. Tell me it doesn't ring true — and I ask you to think again and to look into your own heart.

Of course if God *is* saying that, then it is worth hearing. It is the most staggering compliment to woman, the most exalted appreciation of her dignity — by her Creator! — that one can hear. Fanciful and impossible? Not if it is God who says it. Vast encouragement too: if anyone reading this says wistfully to himself or herself "Would that this were so", he or she must know that *God thinks it so,* and that their own perhaps feeble velleity is backed by God's will. This thing is possible; this is how life ought to be lived. Indeed, without spiritual catastrophe and emotional mutilation — speaking generally — this is how it must be lived.

Two interjections. First, the example I give at length refers to a girl. This for two reasons: first because a man can see the thing more clearly when it is stated about a woman, and it is a man who writes; secondly, because of my teenage readers the majority would be girls. But I emphasise that something analogous applies to the male sex. (In writing about

11

women I have no intention of sounding offensively "sexist". It is a fact some women seem to get angry nowadays if they hear a man saying women are beautiful. I'm sorry about that, but I can't help it).

A second interjection is more important. The argument has been put in its bare essentials. It's a blue-print, not a picture. Remember the amount of deliberation and intention — clear-headed, formed, willed, calculated commitment to experience of sexual pleasure — can be very small, or almost totally absent. Here is a boy sexually aroused by the mere proximity of this girl he loves — is he to avoid her? No! Probably he should deepen his relationship with her. He does so, is entitled to do so, because (if he is a good Christian) he is going out with her not because he wants sexual pleasure, but because he likes her. Do people in fact think things out in that way? Probably not unless they've asked about it, pondered it — and too unless they are Christians. But the virtuous and balanced person is likely to know it more or less instinctively. It's not a meaningless distinction, it's all-important.

To conclude this section. The Church, and more fundamentally God, thinks sex is wonderful. The Church does not think sex a degrading animal phenomenon which holy people would do well to avoid. Nor does the Church think it is just for fun. The Church has the mind of the good lover and sees sex as beautiful, wonderful, worth a man giving his life for. It is because it is so precious, so beautiful, that its misuse would be so tragic, and could presumably result in greater disaster.

That said, it must be emphasised that sexual sin is not the worst sort of sin there is. Moreover, as had been said, for many readers the clarity and deliberation of will required for serious sin in this area is — perhaps compared to every other — least likely to be present.

3. Marriage

If you look at marriage there are three very obvious elements:

(i) Sexual pleasure. For the man at least, a very obvious element. Of all pleasures it is perhaps the most extreme and violent. This is what all the talk earlier to do with the "First two Links" was about.

(ii) Love. This obviously is separable from sexual pleasure. (A man can get sexual pleasure from rape — or from self abuse — but there is no love). The Church says that love — "wanting the good for the other person" — must go with sex. If it isn't for the other person's good, the sexual activity *(even in marriage)* would be wrong. It would be wrong for a man to "make love" with his wife if he's drunk, or if she is unwell.

Some "humanists" insist that pleasure alone is a worthy enough motive for sex. Thus, if I have not seen them misquoted, some would wish children to be taught how to masturbate — not simply for the sake of the present pleasure they experience, but so that later on they would indulge in promiscuous sex without feeling guilt.

There is a biological 'reason' for love, obviously. If strong emotion, enduring tenderness, ties the lovers together, then the chance of them staying together is stronger. And for the sake of the protection of the children, at the very least for their emotional good and stability, it is vital the parents should be together — and happily together.

(iii) Life. Here is the fundamental biological 'reason' for sexual pleasure. If there were not pleasure in sex, presumably no species would breed. (Just as presumably if there were no pleasure in eating, sub-rational species would die of starvation).

The *biological* reason . . . the actual *motive* for love-making presumably is something different! It is not suggested that couples are expected to make love thinking "let's try

13

to beget an heir tonight . . . ''

Here lies the root of the birth-control debate. Granted love should go with sex, should the "life" element be present always ("open-ness to life")? And test-tube babies: here is *life* being started, but the "love" and the "sex" element . . . ? The Church's position in both is that the three elements must go together, that no act of intercourse should not be "open to life", and that every act of generation should be "human" (in the sense that fertilisation should be in the "right place" and in the "right way").

Later, in chapter 4, there are some words about the so-called *three ends* of marriage, and a little about family planning and homosexuality.

The three elements so far could be discussed endlessly, but at least it is clear that they could reasonably be seen to be appropriate in any love between man and woman. But the next one is only visible to Catholics.

(iv) Sacrament. In every sacrament there is a long term effect. In three (Baptism, Confirmation, Priesthood) Catholics believe that the effect lasts for eternity. In the other four, it lasts for a more or less measurable period. In marriage, it lasts as long as the marriage lasts — as long as both their bodies last.

What happens is that when Christ touches the couple when they wed (and he does this in a Sacrament — through his Body, the Church) they are altered. They are given extraordinary power over each other. Already we have seen that *sex* is taken over by *love;* that the two should be open to *life*. Now we see a fourth beauty: Christ operates through each party in the act of love, and as they embrace, express love, perhaps conceive new life, **they actually make each other holy.** Something material, their bodies, has been empowered by Christ in his Church to be the vehicle of Christ's touch. And this power is open to them as long as they live: a sublime heightening of what we have in common with the animals: a glorious compliment paid by Christ to his Father's creation.

And this sanctifying power which is the long-term effect, called in this and other sacraments "sacramental grace", is probably not exercised simply in sexual intercourse. *Any* sign of love, any act that helps the couple and their life together (a kiss, cooking a meal, bathing the baby, going to work) probably has the same effect. These things in Christian marriage (that is, when both are baptised) are not just acts which are "nice" or "helpful" — they *"make the other holy",* probably in the same sort of way which prayer for the partner would open him or her to grace, but in a prayer of a very special sort.

What an inexpressibly wonderful and beautiful gift is Christian marriage! But there is a fifth and final element. And here we are into deep mystery.

(v) Sign. Eph 5:25-33: "You who are husbands must show love to your wives, as Christ showed love to the Church when he gave himself up on its behalf. He would hallow it, purify it by bathing it in the water to which his word gave life; he would summon it into his own presence, the Church in all its beauty, no stain, no wrinkle, no such disfigurements; it was to be holy, it was to be spotless. And that is how a husband ought to love his wife, as if he were loving his own body; in loving his wife, a man is but loving himself. It is unheard of, that a man should bear ill-will to his own flesh and blood; no, he keeps it fed and washed; and so it is with Christ in his Church; we are limbs of his body; flesh and bone we belong to him. That is why a man will leave his father and mother and cling to his wife, and the two will become one flesh. Yes, these words are a high mystery, and I am applying them here to Christ and his Church. Meanwhile, each of you is to love his wife as he would himself, and the wife is to pay reverence to her husband".

A high mystery indeed. One might think, poetically, that

the union of sex was an image of God's love (as the Milky Way is an image of his immensity). But the Holy Spirit through St Paul is saying more than that. At the least, surely it means that every time the Christian couple act as man and wife in conformity with God's law, they are involved somehow in Christ's "wedding" to the human race, to the Church: ultimately, in the Incarnation. Presumably it also means that when sexual differentiation appeared — aeons ago in most primitive life forms — that blind striving was related to the Incarnation of God millions of years in the future. Certainly it means that human love and marriage depend for authenticity on the Love which made God incarnate in Mary's womb. The implications, as in anything to do with God, as in any "mystery", are endless.

It is here as a "sign", that the essential beauty in sex lies. I have numbered it as the fifth component. But it is really the first and the fundamental. It is here that the permanence of marriage takes root and it is here that the essential evil in any misuse of sex resides.

To sum it all up with a diagram:

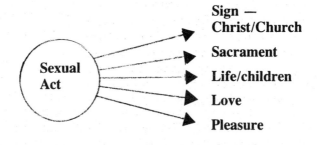

Sexual Act

Sign — Christ/Church

Sacrament

Life/children

Love

Pleasure

Three:

Consecrated Chastity and the single state

1. 'Single' spirituality

Leaving aside motive, the obligations of someone with a vow of chastity are basically the same for anyone not married, save that someone without a vow who aims to marry may properly enter circumstances which would be quite wrong for one who is consecrated. The asceticism required in life would be the same, and the rewards could be the same. The canonical state, of course is different; but the fidelity to God will feel the same: to put it crudely and negatively, a man handling a temptation against the 6th commandment would feel the same whether he was a monk or a marine. Therefore 'singles' who read what follows must translate 'consecrated person', 'vow of chastity' and the rest of the terms which apply to themselves. It would be tedious to spell it out in print.

2. Why consecrated chastity?

Read again the essential points, the positive elements, stated earlier about marriage. Isn't it obvious that if marriage is as wonderful as that, then consecrated chastity must be even more wonderful? For surely God could not encourage us to it unless it were good advice. And he does encourage us to it although his plan in sex is inexpressively beautiful. He encourages the complete and permanent sacrifice of any deliberate sexual pleasure or activity ("Take this" — the making yourselves into *eunuchs* — "you whose hearts are large enough for it'', Mt 19:12). And this seems to rule out every one of the five elements involved in marriage.

See the diagram again. On the left is now described what seems to be the brutal denial of all the good things:

Nothing visible at all   x . . . . → **Sign Christ/Church**

Deprivation of one of the seven Sacraments   x . . . . / . . → **Sacrament**

Sexual Act

Sterility   x . | → **Life/children**

Unable to devote self where heart leads   x . . . . → **Love**

Vowed away under pain of sacrilege   x . . . . → **Pleasure**

What then can be the positive values? Let us start from the top down.

(i) Sign. There are different sorts of signs. An "extrinsic" sign could be a picture, or a "conventional" sign (like a red light as a sign that a car should stop). A crucifix, of course, would be a "picture" sign of Calvary. But you can have another sort of sign, an "intrinsic" one. Here, the sign of the car stopping would be the squeal of tyres and the pressure in the brake-foot; and the sign of Calvary could be — the Mass.

You see the differences: the Mass *is* Calvary; the sound of the tyres *is* the car stopping. Now, the theory — the best guess — is that consecrated chastity is not a "picture sign" of Christ wedding the human race, but *it is the very way He does it*.

Of course any Religious reading this will protest "My vow

of chastity is not the cause of the Incarnation''. No, you are not the ''cause'' of the Annunciation to Our Lady, of the beginning of Redemption: but you are a constituent and active part of the on-going process. In the detonation that occurred when God became man, he has you as part of the flame.

If this is true (and I don't know how you can prove it: you see it or you don't; you listen to the tradition and the magisterium or you don't) then the value of chastity is incalculable. Much may depend on your chastity and mine. If we are 'prophets' (and it would seem that at Final Vows the Church equivalently corroborates the fact that we are such, and designates us so, and commissions us officially to act as such) then our acts have value over and above their obvious worth.

For a prophet is not necessarily one who foretells the future, but one who says (for instance) ''As I do this, now, so — believe me — God will do *thus* to Israel''. God's act on Israel and his impelling the prophet to word or action are part of the same process. (There isn't space to elaborate all this. Religious will doubtless be familiar with this sort of talk. Of course, these things sound more mystical, and more plausible, in a foreign language — preferably French. But we must do the best we can).

At the least, your vow of chastity is working something in the Church: maybe someone's marriage is going to survive; maybe someone in severe temptation may be helped; maybe at the moment of death someone may be able to accept God's love . . .

(ii) Sacrament. Have Religious been deprived of a Sacrament? If so, what are they missing? The answer is, nothing. By their consecration they are allowing the Christ-life in them to be lived out the way Christ lived it, as literally as may be. They are living their Baptism out in the way that is, so to speak, logical. They have appropriated it by way of sacrifice — enabling our Lord to have the chance of more

19

"freedom" in his use of them. They do not need a sacrament in order to "have" their Baptism totally: the married person is brought to that adaptability with the Sacrament of Matrimony: the consecrated don't need that.

(iii) Life. No children! (Again one says — it had better be good, if I am deprived of this!) The clue lies along the lines (it is not a play on words) that Jesus gave up his life to give life to others. Sacrifice of good things, ultimately of self, is at the heart of redemption. As one holy person put it: 'God said to Adam "Go forth and multiply and fill the earth". He has said to me: "Go out and fill the earth too": I *know* I am spiritually fruitful'. Notice that Mt 19:12's "for love of the Kingdom" could mean, minimally, "out of desire to spread the Kingdom".

(iv) Love. Of course we are to love everybody; but sometimes, one feels, one would like to restrict the loving to people one likes, and to do it in the way one wants. This is sacrificed. We are not to love exclusively. The reason: so that we may be free and unfettered to love more people (including, often, the tedious and the repulsive). If we were married, the first duty God would require of us would be to the partner. But he wants us to be committed, and deeply, to many others.

(v) Sexual pleasure. God knows we have bodies and nerves and need for joy. If he wants to, and if we allow him, he could make up to us at a deeper level what we have sacrificed for him. (About this, much more follows later).

3. "Better"?

No one reading Chapter Two of this book would reproach me with depreciating the beauty and the value of sex in marriage. Surely I exalted them. I spent several pages saying "Sex and marriage are wonderful". But now must be said clearly what has been implied already, that consecrated chastity and indeed the single state is even more wonderful.

It is not being proposed that every individual who has a vow of chastity is "better" than married people. Not even that *one* of them is. Quite obviously the single state *(experto crede)* brings with it a continued risk of becoming thoroughly selfish, whereas even the average marriage would be a continual life-long school of generosity and unselfishness. But put it this way: the person with a vow of chastity is *luckier* ("beatius vivit" says the Council of Trent) than the married person.

Why luckier? Because the unmarried state approximates more closely to our Lord's advice. Here I repeat a point already made in this chapter in paragraph 2 under "sign". Mt 19:10-12: "At this, his disciples said to him, If the case stands so between man and wife (*sc.* if a man can't get rid of his wife when he wants to!) it is better not to marry at all. That conclusion, he said, cannot be taken in by everybody, but only by those who have the gift. There are some eunuchs, who were born so from their mother's womb, some were made so by men, and some have made themselves so for the love of the kingdom of heaven; take this in, you whose hearts are large enough for it".

At the least our Lord is here saying that to refrain from the deliberate experience of sexual pleasure (to be a "eunuch"), with the right motive, could entitle one to a gift from God not open to all, which "is the condition that corresponds best to the Kingdom". (Lucien Legrand, *Biblical Doctrine of Virginity,* quoted by Dubay, p.38).

The love of the Kingdom can imply a desire to spread it, as has been pointed out in paragraph 2 under "Life" in this chapter. But "for love of the Kingdom" can mean "out of desire to experience the Kingdom". Now the Kingdom is where Christ reigns, where he is therefore to be met and to be experienced. In this case, to be chosen to be "eunuch" is obviously a very desirable condition!

The Church has often in recent years stated the "better".

But probably not loudly enough. Here are some instances:

1965: *(Optatam totius, 10, On training for the priesthood)*: "(Priestly students) should have a proper knowledge of the duties and dignity of Christian marriage, which represents the love which exists between Christ and the Church. They should recognise the *greater excellence* of virginity consecrated to Christ, however, so that they may offer themselves to the Lord with fully deliberate and generous choice, and a complete surrender of body and soul".

1967 *(Sacerdotalis celibatus, 20)*: "Matrimony according to the will of God continues the work of the *first creation* . . . *But Christ, mediator of a more excellent Testament, has also opened a new way,* in which the human creature adheres *wholly and directly* to the Lord, and is concerned only with him and with his affairs; thus, he manifests in a *clearer and more complete way* the profoundly transforming reality of the New Testament". *(Sacerdotalis celibatus, 23)*: "(Chastity) then is the mystery of the newness of Christ, of all that he is and stands for; it is the *sum of the highest ideals of the Gospel and of the Kingdom". (Sacerdotalis celibatus, 54)*: "The deepest reason for dedicated celibacy is, as we have said, the choice of a *closer and more complete relationship* with the mystery of Christ and the Church for the good of mankind: in this choice there is no doubt that those *highest human values are able to find their fullest expression".*

1970 *(Mos virginis consecrandae,2)*: "Those who consecrate themselves to chastity under the inspiration of the Holy Spirit do so for the sake of a *more fervent love* of Christ and of *greater freedom* in the service of their brothers and sisters".

1971 *(Evangelica Testificatio, 13)*: "Without in any way undermining love and marriage — is not the latter, according to faith, the image and sharing of the union of love joining Christ and the Church? — consecrated chastity evokes this union in a *more immediate way* and brings that *surpassing excellence* to which all human love should tend''.

St Paul, of course, says the same. Difficult for moderns perhaps to read this obscure passage without wincing at the presuppositions, but the message is the Holy Spirit's:

I Cor 7:36-40: "If anyone considers that he is behaving unsuitably towards the girl who is in his charge, on the ground that she is now past her prime, and there is no way of avoiding it, why, let him please himself; there is nothing sinful in it; let her marry. Whereas, if a man remains fixed in his resolution, and makes up his mind to keep the girl who is in his charge unwed, although there is no necessity for it, and he is free to choose for himself, such a man is well advised to give his ward in marriage, and *still better advised* not to give her in marriage. As for a wife, she is yoked to her husband as long as he lives: if her husband is dead, she is free to marry anyone she will, so long as she marries in the Lord. But *more blessed is she, if she remains as she is,* in my judgement; and I, too, claim to have the spirit of God''.

The preceding verses make the same point:

I Cor 7:25-28: "About virgins, I have no command from the Lord; but I give you my opinion, as one who is, under the Lord's mercy, a true counsellor. This then I hold to be the best counsel in such times of stress, that *this is the best condition* for man to be in. Art thou yoked to a wife? Then do not go about to free thyself. Art thou free of wedlock? Then do not go about to find a wife. Not that thou dost commit sin if thou marriest; nor, if she marries, has the virgin committed sin. It is only that those who do so will meet with outward distress. But I leave you your freedom''.

St Paul then goes on — the passage will be cited later — to talk of "the time drawing to an end". His obvious expectation, stated especially in *I Thess 4 and 5,* is that the world would soon end. (Some would say it was Jesus' expectation too). Hence, they go on, the teaching he gives about marriage, and our Lord's too on this and other matters,

23

is an "interim ethic" — the best way to behave in the short interval before it all ends. (After all, if the whole thing is going to blow up soon, why bother?).

To this, these answers could be made. First, the Church absorbed the doctrine and flourished on it: the teaching proved itself, and still does. Secondly, that the Church is coming to terms with the "delayed" end, was able to draw out unrealised implications. Newman suggests that the "delayed" parousia helped the Church to understand something of purgatory: for obviously there were dead hanging around, as it were: presumably with a purpose. So here too a "delayed" resurrection could have been seen to have a connection with chastity, and an important one. Not "don't bother to marry, we'll all be risen soon". But "don't marry: then you'll be anticipating the risen life in chastity". More about this later.

Meanwhile, in the first verses of the same chapter he treats the same question "is it better?"

I Cor 7:1-9: "As for the questions raised in your letter; a man *does well* to abstain from all commerce with women. But, to avoid the danger of fornication, let every man keep his own wife, and every woman her own husband. Let every man give his wife what is her due, and every woman do the same by her husband; he, not she, claims the right over her body as she, not he, claims the right over his. Do not starve one another, unless perhaps you do so for a time, by mutual consent, to leave more freedom for prayer; come together again, or Satan will tempt you, weak as you are. I say this by way of concession; I am not imposing a rule on you. I wish you were all in the same state as myself; but each of us has his own endowment from God, one to live in this way, another in that. To the unmarried, and to widows, I would say that *they will do well to remain in the same state* as myself, but if they have not the gift of continence, let them marry; better to marry than to feel the heat of passion".

But in practice does it work? Is there for instance statistical evidence that a higher proportion of Religious enjoy, shall we say, a more intensely experienced union with God than do a 'control' batch of married people? Well no one has yet performed such a sociological survey. (They will probably get around to it in the USA sooner or later — a PhD thesis in religious sociology, I expect). Who then can give an informed guess? (Or rather, who would be foolhardy enough to stick his neck out?) I believe that priests giving missions and retreats to seculars and to Religious could have an opinion. I would myself guess that a larger proportion of Religious had ''higher'' degrees of experienced union with God in prayer than do the married. One could object at once ''So what? Obviously a working mother with young children cannot give the time to prayer that a nun can''. And indeed the answer maybe as simple as that. And remember we are not talking about *sanctity* . . . But the fact remains that one phenomenon, 'A', seems to be accompanied by another phenomenon, 'B', in a significant manner. Let us not as good empiricists claim a causal connection; nevertheless as a working hypothesis it's fair to say ''If you want B, better try A''. Not that B need be all-important; but if you *do* want it enough to vow A, you are lucky.

4. What is the point?

It is time to amplify the five points of chastity which correspond to the five points of marriage. It is here that the wonder, beauty, privilege, value, utility and risk of chastity lies. Again, then:

(i) Sign

Canon 599 sums up the Church's pondered evaluation: ''The evangelical counsel of chastity embraced for the Kingdom of heaven is a sign of the world to come . . . '' Thus to live ''for the sake of the Kingdom'' will involve not only giving a picture of it, but even making it "begin to happen". There is a hint of this in Mt 22:30: "When the dead rise again, there is to be no marrying and giving in marriage; they are as the angels in heaven are". And this is the implication the Church sees in the "eschatological" remarks of I Cor 7:29-31 alluded to before: "Only, brethren, I would say this: the time is drawing to an end; nothing remains, but for those who have wives to behave as though they had none; those who weep must forget their tears, and those who rejoice in their rejoicing, and those who buy must renounce their possession; and those who take advantage of what the world offers must not take full advantage of it; the fashion of this world is soon to pass away".

You can come to the idea by looking at it this way. Misuse of sex is very terrible; so the right use must be very wonderful: wrong use (say with a prostitute) effects a real union with her — a becoming of "one body". Whereas if one gave one's body to *Christ*, one would effect a "spiritual" union with him — of an intimacy and with effects beyond imagining. And how would one give one's body, make it belong, to Christ? That is a different question; but the preceding steps are clear in St Paul.

1 Cor 6:13-20: "Your bodies are not meant for debauchery, they are meant for the Lord, and the Lord claims your bodies. And God, just as he has raised our Lord from the dead, by his great power will raise us up too. Have you never been told that your bodies belong to the body of Christ? Am I to take what belongs to Christ, and make it one with a harlot? God forbid! Or did you never hear that the man who unites himself to a harlot becomes one body with her? The two, we are told, become one flesh. Whereas the *man who unites himself to the Lord becomes one spirit with him.* Keep clear, then, of debauchery. Any other sin a man commits leaves the body untouched, but the fornicator is committing a crime against his own body. Surely you know that your bodies are

26

shrines of the Holy Spirit, who dwells in you. And he is God's gift to you, so that you are no longer your own masters. A great price was paid to ransom you; glorify God *by making your bodies shrines of his presence"*.

The picture then that begins to emerge is that by using my body (which is a shrine of the Holy Spirit and belongs to Christ) in chastity, I am anticipating the resurrection; indeed since it unites me with the *risen* Christ (the only Christ there is) I am allowing him freedom to act — I am showing the risen life to be effective now. Showing it? *Making* it effective, rather.

(ii) Sacrament

Here it must be shown that my Baptism, the life of Christ in me, is more free to operate when my chastity is given to God.

Canon 604 (stating that virgins — in an 'order' — are recognised as a form of consecrated life) " . . . through their pledge to follow Christ more closely, virgins are consecrated to God, mystically espoused to Christ and dedicated to the service of the Church . . ." Could there be a closer union, could Baptism be more operative, could one be more effective for our Lord than when one is, as it were, deputising for the Church, his Bride in Eph 5? And this is the implication of these words, usually quoted in a different context and for different reasons:

Eph 5: 22-24: "Wives must obey their husbands as they would obey the Lord. The man is the head to which the woman's body is united, *just as Christ is the head of the Church,* he, the saviour on whom the safety of his body depends; and women must owe obedience at all points to their husbands, as the *Church does to Christ"*.

The central work of the Church and first manifestation of Christ's life is of course love. And love it is, of course, that gives rise to chastity, as documents state:

27

Sac. cel. 22: "The motive of the answer (continence) to the divine call is the kingdom of heaven".

Evangelica Testificatio (1971), 13: "Only the love of God, it must be repeated, calls in a decisive way to religious chastity".

And this love which is given, the grace conferred — consequent from baptism — is surely spousal. St Paul takes it for granted his disreputable Corinthians were wedded to Christ: so also is the consecrated celibate:

II Cor 11:2: "My jealousy on your behalf is the jealousy of God himself; I have betrothed you to Christ, so that no other but he should claim you, his bride without spot, and now I am anxious about you".

The person with a vow of chastity must, of all people, assume that Jesus looks on him or her with the obsessive loving tenderness of a spouse absorbed in the beloved.

(iii) Life

St Paul sees that it is in preaching that Christ can fecundate the world. But the imagery he uses and the fact that continence also "speaks" and is prophetic allows us to apply his words to our case:

I Cor 4:15: "Yes, you may have ten thousand schoolmasters in Christ, but not more than one father: it was I that *begot you* in Jesus Christ when I preached the gospel to you".

Chastity is essentially apostolic:

Mt 19:12: Again "for the sake of the Kingdom" can include "for the sake of *spreading* the Kingdom".

Novo incipiente nostro (1979), 8: "Celibacy is a symbol of availability for service".

Sac. cel. 58: "(The celibate priest) has been appointed to act on behalf of men since he is *consecrated completely to*

28

chastity and *to the work* for which the Lord has called him''. So much of what has been said is already merging into the next point:

(iv) Love

I Cor 7:32-35: ''And I would have you free from concern (*sc.* because the fashion of this world is soon to pass away). He who is unmarried is *concerned with God's claim,* asking how he is to please God; whereas the married man is concerned with the world's claim, asking how he is to please his wife; and thus he is at issue with himself. So a woman who is free of wedlock, or a virgin, is concerned with the Lord's claim, intent on holiness, bodily and spiritual; whereas the married woman is concerned with the world's claim, asking how she is to please her husband. I am thinking of your own interest when I say this. It is not that I would hold you in a leash; I am thinking of what is suitable for you, and how *you may best attend to the Lord without distraction''*.

And so, since undistracted love of the Lord is bound to involve it, to the subject of joy.

(v) Joy

For this the sacrifice of the experience of sex is to be thought a little thing. And it seems that this joy, corresponding as it does in our scheme to the joy of sex, is (or could or should be) related to prayer. There seems no escape from this conclusion:

Canon 663: ''The first and principal duty of all religious is to be the contemplation of things divine, and constant union with God in prayer''.

A widow — or presumably anyone who is free in the way a widow was in St Paul's day — is presumed to be ready to pray at night as well:

I Tim 5:5,6. "The woman who is indeed a widow, bereft of all help, will put her trust in God, and spend her time, night and day, upon the prayer and petitions that belong to her state; one who lives in luxury would be alive and dead both at once". (Evidently chastity is largely for prayer — just as poverty is, in St Paul's mind).

Continence *inside marriage* is taken to be appropriate for prayer; and so presumably facility in prayer is one of the hopeful results from consecrated chastity:

I Cor 7:5. "Do not starve one another, unless you do so for a time, by mutual consent, *to have more freedom for prayer".*

In the Gospel sacrifice of sex is not alone in bringing with it untold reward, but it is one of the elements:

Lk 18:29,30. "Jesus said to them I promise you everyone who has forsaken home or parents, or brethren, *or wife, or children* for the sake of the Kingdom of God, will receive, *in this present world,* many times their worth, and in the world to come, everlasting life".

And again, the fundamental verse:

Mt 19:12. "Take this in (the making a eunuch of oneself) for the sake of the kingdom of heaven" as if he said "sacrifice *this* (never having a shoulder to lay your head on, never having anyone to put your arms around) and I will promise you that you will have *me.* I will more than make up for it, for you will know my embrace; for the Kingdom is where I reign and act".

Joy, prayer, love — it is always his gift first. If we are able to give in love it is because he gives us the power. And we need his power:

Evangelica Tesificatio, 7 (quoting *Lumen Gentium, 43*): "Through such a bond (of vows, for example) a person is *totally* dedicated by God to an act of *supreme* love".

And what does God get out of it all? St Peter, speaking to married women, will say that beauty and riches (and sex too, perhaps?) are to be ignored compared with what is really important:

I Pet 3:3,4. "Your beauty must be not in braided hair, not in gold trinkets, not in the dress you wear, but in the hidden features of your hearts, in a possession you can never lose, that is a calm and tranquil spirit; to God's eyes, beyond price". That is what it is all about: to give God something that delights him — "beyond price".

There is a very great danger that the Religious may forget that our Lord undertook a commitment when a vow of chastity was taken. The term "Bride of Christ" is not empty: it is a fact that our Lord — no matter what negligence, betrayal, regret there may be on the part of the Religious — will never be able to look on her save as spouse regarding a tenderly loved bride: or — the nearest imagery we can get for a man — as friend, leader, protector would look on a follower whom he would always see as a comrade.

In other words, the consecrated person insults our Saviour if he or she does not apply to self what every Christian should know is Christ's attitude. And we do, often, forget — when we should be intoxicated with it. Here are familiar texts paraphrased, amplified or made explicit; this is the heart of this booklet, and its whole purpose:

I would call you and call you;
I call you to come to me;
I want you to experience my spirit as a fountain welling up in your heart. (Jn 7:37-39)

The Way you must go — it is *myself;*
The Truth you need — it is *myself;*
I am the Life you must live — everlasting Life in the Father. (Jn 14:6)

The food you need to live forever — *living* substance. (Jn 6:51)

The only light the world needs — *all* the light it needs, is myself. (Jn 9:5)

To you, I will always be as a shepherd who loves his sheep, and is ready to die for any one of them — *for you.* (Jn 10)

The life which will be in you when you rise from the dead — it is *I.* (Jn 11:25)

The spirit whom I give you, he is a tender and loving friend to you, and *cannot be anything else.* (Jn 14:26, 15:26)

The Life you need is Light, and it is in me (Jn 1:4)

I give you power to be child of my Father, of God himself. (Jn 1:12)

I am full of all you need — and I give it to you. (Jn 1:16)

Believe in me and you will live forever. (Jn 3:15)

I will slake your thirst, and the water will be in you like a spring — for ever. (Jn 4:14)

My Father is *your* dear and loving Father too. (Mt 6:9)

You may be selfish and heartless, but my Father will be kind. (Lk 6:35)

I will raise you up to be with me when the time comes. (Jn 6:44)

You have eaten my Flesh and drunk my Blood. (Jn 6:55)

You are now living in me, and I in you. (Jn 6:55-57)

I give Life to whomsoever I wish to; and I give it to you. (John 5:21)

No one will ever snatch you away from me. (Jn 10:28)

Come with me! (Mt 4:19)

Never be frightened! (Lk 12:32)

You're weighed down? Come to me! (Mt 11:28)

Four:

Controversial or painful

1. The "Ends" of marriage

More than once, five "points" have been alleged about marriage and, in a more eminent way, about chastity. And three (sex, love, life) have for many years been spoken of as the "ends" of marriage. Of these "life" was usually described as the primary end, and love/sex as secondary. During Vatican II great interest (and some dismay) arose because the council seemed to omit, quite pointedly, any mention of "primary" or "secondary".

It is an important matter. The Church's position was that the primary end must never be blocked out; that if there were a complete act of sex it had to be "open to life"; that the secondary end (excellent as it is) should never be achieved at the expense of the primary.

If that is so, then artificial birth-control is wrong, for here the primary end is frustrated. For those who wanted a change in the Church's teaching, an important step would be the enhancing of the "secondary" ends at the expense of the primary.

But it is in fact very difficult, in the framework of thought that has guided the Church's thinking for many centuries, not to think of rightness or wrongness as being essentially connected with the use of a thing according to its purpose, according to what it is for, its "primary end". And in fact this insight still remains in Vatican II. *Gaudium et spes, 51* has a footnote 14 in which are listed documents, cited as the source of that "teaching authority of the Church" which we must not disobey. They are *Casti connubii (1930)* and Pope Pius XII's *Address to midwives (1951);* both of them refer to the "ends".

This is not to deny the importance of the love aspect, which (if you look at the matter a different way) could itself be described as "primary". (indeed it's better to say that the "end" is single — but you can look at it in two aspects). For certainly sex is not *only* for conceiving children; love, support, sympathy, forgiveness, joy, pleasure, healing, experience of one's worth — all these are (or should be or could be) truly involved in sexual expression.

One of the prophets of this truth is Dr Jack Dominian, a notable Catholic who has for years been a luminary of the British Catholic Marriage Advisory Council, a guide of the hierarchy and one whose wisdom and sympathy has helped innumerable couples. He is often described as a theologian, and the Catholic press have often enough publicly referred to his insight and spiritual sensitivity. But he seems to be disastrously wrong.

He means (I think) to reject "primary and secondary" classification. But it is interesting that nearly twenty-five years after Vatican II his mind still uses these thought patterns, if only to reject the implications. And his conclusions after rejecting them are momentous. In *New Internationalist, (April 1986)* Dr Dominian writes " . . . has the time come to revoke the prohibition on pre-marital sex, adultery and homosexuality? . . . I believe that a case *can* be made for the traditional view. But I also believe that modifications to the teaching are necessary . . . if sex is *not* just for procreation, if its purpose is also to unite people in love, then one can visualise the day when permanent, loving relationships between homosexuals — homosexual marriages, in other words — may be approved. However, for the time being, the teaching of Christianity appears strong in this matter, and I foresee no early resolution to this question".

My argument therefore is this: even after Vatican II it is

reasonable to think in the categories of primary and secondary ends; and if you do not, however spiritually gifted you may be, you could find yourself apparently advocating abominations.

2. Family Planning

Family Planning is such an important subject that Appendix 1 is devoted wholly to it, with particular reference to Natural Family Planning.

The Church's position, repeatedly reiterated by Paul VI and John Paul II, seems more and more vindicated by the consequences of the "sexual revolution" begun in the 1960s. It is more easily seen now. In 1968 the German and Austrian bishops issued an "explanation" after *Humanae Vitae* which must be understood as saying that the morality of contraception was a matter for private judgement. Eight other European hierarchies also dissented, as did Canada (and Indonesia, with its Dutch bishops). Twenty years later the Austrian bishops withdrew their dissent. One feels many things about this . . . one might be, that it's better to stay with the Pope and the bishops who speak with him. In fact any apparent dissent was put paid to by the Bishops at the International Synod of Bishops on the Family. They unanimously backed *Humanae Vitae*. The Synod Fathers represented their Conferences.

3. Homosexuality

How things have changed since 1944, when the anglican scholar C S Lewis over the radio could speak like this without provoking ridicule and obloquy: "Chastity is the most unpopular of the Christian virtues. There is no way of getting away from it: the Christian rule is: either marriage, with complete faithfulness to you partner, or total abstinence". (*Mere Christianity,* Fontana).

What then of the homosexual? For the sexual urges are

there, but they cannot be given in marriage. The Church describes the state as "disordered", while it readily proclaims that the individual who experiences sexual attraction to members of the same sex may be totally innocent. But — there must be no deliberate experience of sexual pleasure.

Now all this is being stated coldly, baldly — and shortly. It could and should be qualified by compassion, and more understanding than space allows. A homosexual could reasonably protest that he or she is more than an agent of sexual acts: there could be a way of thinking, a way of understanding, a way of sympathising, an appreciation of beauty, a way of loving (not involving sexual expression) that is sensed as specifically belonging to the sexual orientation. Is all *that* wrong? No. It is potentially grace-filled. What is "forbidden" (that is, what is ultimately destructive of self and love) is what is forbidden to the heterosexual: any *deliberate* experience of sexual pleasure outside of marriage or, without overwhelming good reason, emotional involvement likely to lead to it. And why? For the same reason as has been outlined too briefly above: sexual experience is of its nature ordered to the giving of life.

Is this hard for homosexuals to hear? Evidently. But if they can accept God's teaching, as the Church insists it is, a wonder opens up. They are obviously being asked by God, *chosen* indeed by God, to follow what the person with the vow of chastity has been invited to: lifelong, complete chastity, excluding any willed experience of sexual pleasure. Now that is hard (ask any Religious); but let no-one say it is not "promotion" in God's Kingdom.

But surely the Religious chose it, the homosexual had it imposed? I wonder . . . was not the chaste Religious *chosen* by God to it? Are not the circumstances that led to the homosexual's "disordering", willed or at least permitted by God, just as clear a choosing?

Not that the homosexual should be encouraged to enter Religious life or the Priesthood. The conditions are likely to prove too heavy a burden to permit a vow of chastity. But the vocation to chastity would indeed seem clearly to be an invitation from God: and if he asks a particular fulfilment of his will he *must* will to give the grace — that is, he must at least will the subject to pray (to live therefore) in a way that will inevitably open him or her to the necessary grace.

There is much talk about homosexuality today. Probably too much, in the sense that many young people are likely to begin to believe they are homosexual when in fact they are not.

Some say the proportion of homosexuals among men would be 10%. Others say the number is far less; or that many homosexuals have as it were "trained themselves" so to be. It would seem that the figures obtained from polls would vary greatly depending on the definition of the terms. It could be said that if society is inclining people to homosexuality (by altering sexual expectations, by education, by propaganda) the true number of those congenitally predisposed to homosexuality might be very small.

Consider a society in a different age: England in the mid 18th century. And in a society in which one might think conditions could impel young men towards homosexual activity: the Navy during the Seven Years war. N A M Rodger in *The Wooden World, an Anatomy of the Georgian Navy* (Fontana 1988) writes: " . . . a question beloved of some modern historians, the incidence of homosexuality . . . There appear in fact to have been eleven courts martial for so doing during the war, of which four led to acquittals, and seven convictions on lesser charges . . . (this in) a sea-going population which was for most of the war seventy or eighty thousand, but the crime was strongly abhorred . . . All these cases, (*sc.* including probably more among officers), add up to a very insignificant total; a score or so of known instances, over a period of nearly nine years during which at least a hundred thousand individuals must have served in the Navy. It is difficult to believe that there can have been any serious problem with a crime so much detested, but so seldom mentioned. If senior officers were concerned about it, they gave no hint of the fact in their correspondence''. And he points out that an 18th century warship would be the most impossible place to conceal the business.

Why all this about the Navy between 1755 to 1763? Because if someone who reads this thinks he is a homosexual, he could do well to think again; he may be wrongly convinced. And if he or she *is* homosexual, then as has been said, he must consider himself chosen (by *God*) to the austere, lovely, sacrificial, endlessly fulfilling and apostolic love of perfect chastity. What a tragedy if he or she were talked out of accepting that privilege!

4. Confused?

Perhaps this is too much on homosexuality. But it is of present (1989) concern. The Church's teaching is not in doubt, but the dissemination of the teaching can be difficult. In 1988 the hierarchy of England and Wales commissioned a video, ''A Time to Embrace''. Most Catholic secondary schools were sent a copy, with a £25 invoice. Praised by many bishops and their spokesmen, the video caused anxiety to some. If there was a weakness it might be due to pedagogical considerations: ''The video scenes . . . do not themselves provide the values and answers'' (to the realistic situations). ''We are also certain that the video should not amount to a lecture or 'talking heads' recitation of the Church's teaching . . . '' Thus the preface to the accompanying teachers' guide.

This could fuel the anxiety of those who felt that in this instance the Church's teaching might be being implicitly denied by a conniving silence. So too could the fact that the talented non-Catholic media expert prominently involved in producing the video said in the weekly *Catholic Herald* (Feb 1989) that in the part on homosexuality she had contrived an "honourable fudge"; her own views on the Church's teaching are that the Church "would rather meet a gay man weeping in the confessional after a sordid and possibly dangerous one-night stand, than encourage him to build a sustaining, intimate relationship".

A press release from *Quest* (Nov 1988), a Catholic organisation for homosexuals, applauded the video. "The discerning teacher, well supported by the manual, will wisely encourage pupils to understand that the homosexual person is no different from the heterosexual experiencing a loneliness that impels him to find someone to love and to share life with".

Thus in this instance the teaching provided by the local Church seemed to be acceptable to those who would condone homosexual acts. And if the teaching *here* is confused, or divergent from the Roman Magisterium, what may be the situation in less extreme matters?

But one must accept that Bishops may have to use people, for their professional expertise, who for one reason or another are not able to support the Church. And one can hardly demand that Bishops should endlessly correct their own experts. The practical conclusion must be, again: when in doubt, stay with the Pope; it is (thank God) a practical impossibility that the hierarchy (probably *any* hierarchy) could intend dissent from Rome.

There is a further source of confusion in sexual matters. Not simply "Has the Church changed its teaching?" (It hasn't). But "How can God's law be lived?" (This is an old difficulty, the former one is new). People vary immensely in their susceptibility to sexual pressures: for some, at some time in their lives, observance of God's law seems an almost impossible burden.

"Concupiscence" is the technical term for disoriented desire for pleasure. It lies at the root of disordered sex. The ultimate and fundamental solution to the problem of handling overpowering desires for pleasure would be, I suppose, an

39

even stronger taste for pleasure in, from, God. A treatment of *sufficient* and *sacramental grace*, showing that it can overcome concupiscence (if incompletely in this life) is in order. It won't be attempted. But the next chapter may help.

Five:

The Mass

1. Importance

The Mass is not only the centre of our Faith, it is the moment when heaven penetrates this world and it makes us present — truly and in reality — to Christ as he was on Calvary and at the moment of the Resurrection.

The difficulty, of course, is that while we *know* this is true, we do not feel it. But as with so much of life, here too we have to disregard the unhelpful feelings and to live in the light of what we know. Of course, if 'feelings' can help, then we use them; and more and more since the renewal of the liturgy after Vatican II we have done our best to make active and intelligent participation in the mystery as possible as may be — even to children.

But it *is* a mystery. Canon 899 reminds us ''the Eucharist is an action of Christ himself and of the Church. In it Christ the Lord, through the ministry of the priest, offers himself, substantially present under the appearances of bread and wine, to God the Father . . . '' Who could exhaust the meaning of that? Or the importance? And the Council speaks of the liturgy, more than once, as ''the summit toward which the activity of the Church is directed: it is also the fount from which all her power flows. For the goal of apostolic endeavour is that all who are made the sons of God by faith and baptism should come together and praise God in the midst of his Church, to take part in the Sacrifice and to eat the Lord's Supper''. How can one comprehend what gives meaning to the whole of life — perhaps the whole of creation?

"Christ offers himself" . . . "the fount of the Church's power". Perhaps the easiest elaboration of this is available in the Pope's document *Dominicae Cenae* of 1980; the shortest, clearest plea against abuses (which are many, varied, deeply injurious to unity and often indicative of radical ignorance of doctrine) is in *Inaestimabile Donum* of 1980. The first part of this chapter seeks to "explain" the Mass and to counter abuse.

2. The essential insight?

There are innumerable ways of looking at the Mass. What I give here is only one way. It leaves out clear emphasis on the community aspect; on the implications of the paschal meal; on ways of participating; and on much else. But it does pick out the essential. Please read carefully, several times, the next two paragraphs.

The night before he died Jesus Christ said, more or less: "Listen, you who are my close friends: I tell you now that *this* (he points to the bread) is my Living Body; and *this* (he points to the wine) is my Living Blood. Now, *do this* (that plainly is an order) and every time you do — you will be present to my Living Body and my Living Blood *as it will be for you tomorrow, when I die on the Cross".*

Jesus Christ, who is God, has thus devised a way of making what happened in history nearly two thousand years ago on Calvary happen . . . here! now! And *why* would he want us to be present with him at Calvary (present *in fact* that is, not present in imagination or through a sort of pious mime)? Well, two reasons come to mind very easily. First, companionship: he did not have many *friends* with him on Calvary — but at Mass he can have you and me! And that surely is a joy to Jesus Christ and to his Mother . . . But there is a second reason. If he can have you and me *really* with him at Calvary, when he returns to his Father (" . . . when he returns to his Father?" . . . present then also at the moment of the *Resurrection*) well then — *we are saved!* The Mass really *is* the work of our Redemption: there is nothing more important, nothing more costly, nothing more beautiful. If we can be with him at Calvary, with him in the garden of the Resurrection (not just physically present, but willed to him, welded to him, wedded to him) then his work for us is achieved. Of course, because we need to be with him at Calvary, at the moment of the Resurrection (and of the Ascension, and of Pentecost . . . all that is involved in his return to his Father, in his Passover), and because we live in space and time, we need to reiterate our decision; Mass is not something we are to do just once. He "ever lives to make intercession for us": the Mass is a way of reaching him in his moment of intercession.

3. 'Obligation'

And that is the reason for the obligation to go to Mass on Sundays and days of Obligation. It is not that the Church is laying down a rule so much that she is making a statement of fact: "Look, either you believe what I say about the Mass, or you don't. If you don't believe, then you have lost the Faith. If you do believe, and you cannot be bothered to go (not 52 times in the year, on the Lord's day, and a handful of other days) . . . well then, your heartlessness seems almost worse. Can't you see it's important?" That is what the Church means when it says "You've got to go to Mass on Sundays".

Notice that the Mass 'works' not because you and I are praying (though our prayer is a condition for receiving the gifts God wants to give), but because *Christ is present.* The Mass is not a prayer service over a bit of blessed bread — used as a symbol of our unity together and of the body of Christ; *the living Christ is actually and actively present.* (And it is *not* a bit of blessed bread, it is Jesus in the moment of his return to his Father.)

It is knowledge of these facts that makes the Mass an

43

addiction for the informed Catholic — the sweetest addiction there is. And of course although a slovenly priest celebrating the Mass, or an irreverent liturgy, or banal music, or vacuous sermons, or a headache, or a million other things may be annoying (or even scandalous), they cannot destroy the value of the Mass. The Mass gives perfect glory to God, and perfect praise to the Father, because it is Christ's work. Neither you or I, nor the priest, can spoil it. And a good motive for going? . . . *what Jesus Christ gets out of it;* not what I get out of it. (And certainly not what I *feel* I get out of it). It is, in short, a love response of ours as well as God's.

4. The 'shape'

It can be useful, when taking part in the Mass, to keep in one's mind the basic structure.   That way it is easier to recall one's wandering attention and, by opening oneself to the "attitude" appropriate to that part of the Mass, resume a closer participation. (Sophisticated readers must here permit an elaboration of what is often taught to children).

The Mass is in two parts — a Liturgy of the Word, and a Liturgy of the Eucharist — with (as one may envisage it) a space in between. Each of these two parts has two movements: one 'up' to God, and one 'down' from God. The whole becomes a sort of 'M' shape (see next page).

The Liturgy of the Word, at least on a Sunday, takes most of the time. Boredom? Yes, if one does not know how to listen to God's Word, if one does not love the Bible; perhaps if one has not prayed the readings over beforehand, if one has not acquired the knack of prayer . . . Catholics who say they get bored at Mass are really saying that their spiritual life is weak in these areas. (Of course, in the second part of the Mass it would be impossible to be bored once one knew what was happening, and providing one believed it).

LITURGY OF THE WORD   EUCHARISTIC LITURGY

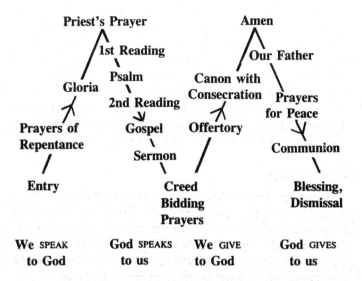

| We SPEAK to God | God SPEAKS to us | We GIVE to God | God GIVES to us |

5. Union with God

Those who cannot go to Communion, for *whatever* reason, should never feel it is not worth going to Mass. But it is true the normal consummation of our presence at Calvary and the moment of the Resurrection, of our will to identify ourselves with Christ's gift of himself to the Father, would be to go to Communion. There are innumerable overtones to this action, and they must have been present — and must be present now — to the mind of Christ. There is the "making of unity" with our fellow guests at the feast. The pledging ourselves to our Host, and the glad acceptance of his responsibilities towards us (one remembers the implications in the Middle East, even today, of having taken food and drink in someone's house). The union with not just the guests and the Host, but with the Victim; the being-built-into-Christ as well as the "receiving" of what he has to give. The intended union with all God's people who celebrated the

45

Pasch throughout the ages. The realisation that there are spousal and nuptial — frankly sexual — overtones: "the union I want with you", says Jesus, "I can only express by using food symbolism; I cannot use sexual symbolism as the pagan religions did; I will go beyond that and I will say to you, 'do not simply embrace Me, consume my Living Body and Blood' ". To put it simply: we give great joy to the Sacred Heart.

All this, of course, depends on the Real Presence. The Mass "works" not because you and I are praying, but because Christ is truly present.

But the major "work" in the Mass is in the movement "we give to God". We give, on Sunday, money . . . money is work, skill, sweat, sacrifice — it is, in a way, a bit of one's self, one's life, that one is giving. And it is in fact one's *whole* self one is meant to give — money or not, Sunday or not. One's prayers, works, actions, joys, sufferings; one's loves and cares; one's failures and sins; all the content of one's heart. Most of all, one's love. Active participation in the Mass *(actuosa participatio)* does not mean primarily movements or words — it means total, internal, willed, union with Christ's sacrifice; a process that begins long before I enter the church door.

All this gift of self is symbolised by bread and wine — which need so much work to produce. And something utterly wonderful happens to this bread and wine: God takes over, and it becomes the Living Christ. And what you and I brought to the Mass is swept up in Christ's action, and brought before the throne of the Father.

The Church always encourages prayer before the Blessed Sacrament. It is prayer before the Risen Christ in person, for the value of the Blessed Sacrament lies in the fact that It is what It is because of the Mass at which It was consecrated. Every aspect of the Eucharistic devotion can and should be a thanksgiving for the last Mass one was present at, and an anticipation of the next. Devotion to the Blessed

Sacrament is normally commensurate with the understanding of the Mass; and if I want to love the Mass more, a good starting point would be to pray more — before the Blessed Sacrament. Certainly to make little of the reserved Sacrament implies a misunderstanding of the Mass. "Visits", Holy Hours, Benediction, the "saluting" of the real Presence when passing a church — all these are important in our love affair with God.

A very useful work, if enough volunteers can be collected, is to form a "Prayer Guard" for a church which has to be kept locked. If enough people agree to pray and guard, in twos, for half an hour or an hour at a time, then a church can be kept open — often for hours each day. It is a sad fact that since the sixties most churches have had to be shut for fear of vandalism.

6. The Blessed Sacrament — what?

As to what happens at consecration, what has effected this extraordinary Presence, no one can adequately explain. The Church's position is that if you are using the language of scholastic philosophy and theology, only one term is possible: transubstantiation. This worries some people. It need not. (If you understand what hylemorphism is; can explain *actus* and *potentia*; explain what a *substantia* is and an *accidens*, only then need you worry if you do not want to use the term "transubstantiation" of the Sacrament. Not otherwise). In the language of of other philosophies, terms other than Transubstantiation would have to be used. The mind of the teaching Church and of the Pope would seem to be that other philosophies do not appear to be such useful tools as is scholasticism for handling most theological concepts, including those to do with the Blessed Sacrament.

Still, they can and should be used, and they can give insights. But beware words like "Transfinalisation" and "Transignification". If these words mean "the end and purpose of this material is no longer that it should be treated as bread, but as the Body of Christ''; and, ''this material *means* to me, no longer bread, but the Body of Christ'' — then one can be in confusion. The point is: how does *God* see it? If *he* sees it and treats it as Christ's Body, then it *is*. Remember that an unbeliever receiving communion receives Christ's Body. He may get no union with God, no grace, from it, but it is still Christ's Body; that Body is there independently of his belief. If everyone in the world disbelieved, the angels and saints would still be in adoration before each tabernacle.

7. How?

Does all this matter? For two reasons it does. First, because the Church, as always seeing deeper through response to mistaken views, has committed itself to proclaiming certainty — at least in some respects — as to what has happened in the Eucharist. Secondly, because accepting the truth opens you to an awareness of the sheer size of what is happening, God has invented a whole new order of being. Not content with the extraordinary and mysterious universe of science and history, or with the ''spiritual'' world of heaven outside space and time, He has devised an utterly mysterious compenetration of the two — the Sacramental Order. And in *this* Sacrament, the material world has not just become a sign, but the very vehicle of God's presence.

Some people would prefer not to think about this sort of thing, and feel that mysteries should be left in decent obscurity. But if they do so, before long they find themselves talking of dogma as being only the ''shell'' inside which lies the kernel of truth, and trying to exegete away certainties the Church has in fact proclaimed. This is a mistake. We can all sympathise with Elizabeth I when she dismissed a world of controversy so simply and prettily:

"His were the lips that spake it
He took the bread and brake it
And what his word doth make it
So I believe and take it."

And of course, we can all say that. But the point is that we do know more, a little more, about what "His word makes it"; and it is no compliment to Him to duck the issue. And no help to ecumenism to fudge our own beliefs.

"His word" made his true human presence, body, blood and soul, be there for us. And with it, of course, his Godhead. No bread remains. He does *not* use the atoms and molecules of carbon, hydrogen, starch and so forth as a means of making himself present — a sort of re-constitution of his body; they are an indication that he is there (where the recognisable fragment of the Host, or drop of the contents of the chalice, there *is* his real and true (and human) Presence. The atoms and molecules of carbon and the rest remain. But they are not the Body of Christ — they only indicate, now, that he is present there).

So we have here the materials of bread existing without any bread, and the Body of Christ present — without of course any of *its* materials detectable.

Just as matter and space seem to be here confused (*all* Christ is present in every consecrated Host, and in every identifiable fragment of it) so is motion. The atoms and molecules of bread (although there is no bread!) move; the Body of Christ does not. Place too: the Host is in your mouth, so is the whole risen Body of Christ; but it does not touch your tongue — only the atoms and molecules of "breadiness" do that.

All mysteries of religion are inexaustible, but they are invitations to see further into God, not "no go" signs. It may be that the mystery of the real Presence throws a little light on the mystery of our Lord's risen body. One thing is sure, if God can become incarnate, we ought not to be surprised what he does with matter after that event.

If one avoids the *fact* of transubstantiation, one is left with symbols only. And the reality of the Presence is likely to become no more than poetry, and the Mass a prayerful mime. There *is* symbolism in the Blessed Sacrament. But it is not precisely the Living Christ who is symbolised — he *is there:* it *is* the Lamb of God. The Church of England used to say the Reality we believe in "quite overthroweth the nature of a sacrament". We say: No, the sign is there (it must be in a sacrament, but working at another level).

For all this there is of course ultimately no evidence at all except the word of the Church. To say that John teaches it is to insult all learned Protestants: it is the Catholic Church that says this is how to interpret John 6 (indeed, we would say, it is the Church that wrote John 6). The converse of this is, of course, the lovely fact that if you can believe the fact of Blessed Sacrament as the Church has made it explicit (for which astounding, bizarre belief there is no evidence whatever except the Church's word) — if you can manage to believe *that* — then there is really nothing the Church could teach which you oughtn't to be able to accept . . . in other words, *you believe!* The Blessed Sacrament really is the crux of faith. A genuflection to It, an incensation, the priest's words as he holds the Host "This is the Lamb of God", is either appalling and obscene blasphemy, or worship of the Living God here present.

Six:

Do I really think God is Lovable?

1. The problem of evil

The strongest case against God, and the one that in practice often makes atheists, is this. If God were all-powerful, he *could* stop all suffering and all evil: if he were all good, he *would* stop it. But God does allow suffering and evil. Therefore God is either not all-powerful or not all-good. Therefore God does not exist.

Notice that any suffering, any ugliness, any horror suffices — a squashed bird in the road, a weeping child, is enough: it does not have to be cancer or a nuclear holocaust. But add up the millennia and total the agony, and the case looks a strong one.

Here is the best answer I know. It's the traditional Christian one. (Of course, if you don't believe in the devil, it won't hold for you; but then I do write for traditional Christians, and specially for those faithful to Rome). But the subject is a mystery, and the "explanation" of course, only shifts the question further back. That is the most one can ever do with mystery. Take it in three stages:

(i) Hell. The worst evil that can be conceived. But it exists not because God is cruel, but because he is good. Being good, he gives good gifts. One is that we live for ever; another that we can love. But to love (that is, to will the good — not just to feel affection) we must be able to choose. And to choose we must (at least sometimes) be free.

But being free we could choose evil. It could be possible

51

to choose so badly that we mutilate ourselves spiritually, to the extent that when we see God, we would find him hateful. Living for ever, we would be endlessly fixed, through our own choice, in hatred of the One who alone could give us bliss.

Looked at thus, Hell is the result of our own bad choice; and God can do nothing about it — unless he over-rides our free choice, or annihilates us: but this would be a contradiction in God's will.

(ii) Suffering on earth

(a) Most suffering on earth (all the wars, all the results of vice, all the quarrels . . .) is due to bad choices of men, resulting from sin, or stupidity ultimately resulting from sinfulness. Thus, like Hell, all this suffering results from the misuse of one of God's good gifts, namely freedom.

(b) There is a residue of suffering on earth, and a large residue, which cannot be blamed on the misuse of human freedom. Animal suffering before man appeared, or which is not caused by man; natural disasters; disease when it is not due to human sin or stupidity.

But this too is possibly reducible to the misuse of freedom: not human, but angelic. If Satan were in some fashion the "guardian angel" of this world, a lot would be explained. When he fell, God did not annihilate him. He still has intellect, power and some sort of stewardship over the world (or this solar system, or this galaxy . . .). But he is now fixed in malevolence against God and against everything that speaks to him of God, very much including man.

Satan cannot create. Only God does that. But Satan can distort God's creation. We ourselves can do that; he could do it much more deeply and much more intimately. Here could be the reason for these things that seem so horrible in nature: parasitism, the deathly conflict among all forms of life, the cruelty in nature. Here could be the reason for "natural" evil — where suffering occurs which is not due to human sin or stupidity.

Faced with suffering then it would seem the instinct to shake our fist at the sky and cry "This *should not* have happened", is a perfectly natural and proper one. But we should shake our fist at the right person. It is not God who is to blame. Satan is the enemy. God indeed became man and bled and died to put all this — all that now seems ugly — right.

2. Need for a healing

The chronic temptation for all of us is to think God does not love us. Only the most primitive and ignorant Christian (there are lots of them) would put it into words, but it is there, in all of us. The temptation not to trust him. If we *really* believed he was all-good, and was all-powerful — present to us in every incident and every moment, and present with total love and good intent — we would nearly be in paradise.

There would be no agony about the past, no dread of the future; no normal irritation, no fear, no anxiety, no anger in the present. How could there be, if we really understood that the living God was totally in control of every event, and totally loving? True, Jesus was in agony, and in the garden in agony over a future event. And he was in no doubt about his Father. The point is that though we will not be excused pain (physical, mental, psychological) our reaction to these pains would be totally different. As was Christ's. God seems to have allowed the darkness of Gethsemane — there were things proper to us which he had to endure if they were to be redeemed and become redemptive for us — but he mastered them. And the peace, the seeming "control" of events which was his normal state, would presumably be ours: *if* we really knew he really loved us.

A test: can we *praise* and *thank* God for *everything?*

Our problem is perhaps less viciousness than blindness. We don't see, we don't know. Of course we are partly to blame, for sin has made it all worse; failure in loving — in the will — has influenced the failure to know — in the intellect. But the truth is that this root defect in us (how much would be cured in us if we *really* knew we were *really* loved, and by such a Father!) is in intellect, not will. It is not a question of saying to ourselves "Try Harder! If you loved more, you would know he loved you" (For some, disastrously, that turns into "Lord, will you love me if I *earn* your love?" Ultimately: "God, I will save myself"!) It is rather: "Lord, I know you love me, but I don't *experience* it. Lord, you've got to show me in ways I can understand".

And so, not surprisingly, we are in the state, as usual, of asking for a grace. Grace is gift: a gift is something you thank for, you can use, you can abuse, you can lose, you can ask for — but you can never earn. What is doctrinally certain is that God will certainly give us the gift and grace to pray for what we need; and such prayer he would surely mean to answer.

There are some prayers that he cannot *not* answer, and in which he tells us publicly he *is* answering. These are the Sacraments. And the Sacraments, rightly understood and used, cover every human need. But foolishly one feels one might have wished that God, who, when I present my sin in a sense *publicly* to Christ's Church in Confession, forgives (perhaps by lifting my sorrow to a new level of love) and even brings me closer to himself because of my very weakness, might have provided a sacrament for healing: a sacrament mid-way, as it were, between Confession (for sin) and Anointing (for life-threatening illness). A sacrament where I could present my hurts and wounds — wounds I may have received without sin on my part, or anyone else's — to the priest as minister of the Church and Christ's representative . . . and with the Blessed Sacrament exposed! In that context I express my belief in Christ's power, and the priest prays, anoints (with oil blessed ordinarily, not the consecrated oils) and blesses me.

There isn't a sacrament for this. But Christ must *want* to heal us, and a service using "sacramentals" is outlined in the Appendix 2.

These wounds do not only threaten my experienced knowledge of God's love of me, they can damage me in many ways. The perfectly innocent mistakes or even the unconscious attitudes of parents can result, psychiatrists will tell, in lifelong crippling. And so of course can hurts done to us culpably. And the wounds we receive from injuries done to people or things we love. And the self-inflicted wounds: the guilts from our own sins and failures. All these mark us, constrict us, can cripple us.

Presumably the first step to being healed is to realise that God was present in the wounding event, and is present in every throb and pulse and neurotic twinge that results. How present? Because no movement of a single atom, no pulse of energy, no least change in a nerve synapse takes place without God's enabling power and without his will. But God became man; the second Person of the Blessed Trinity is humanly aware of and present in each of these least events. Jesus *is there* in the agony. All that has to be done is to open this event to him as saviour, and it is transformed.

The 'healing' is almost incidental, for the horror is redeemed. Jesus has now conquered in what seemed to be Satan's territory; what was the enemy's victory has been dashed out of his hand. In "Ways of Forgiveness" in this series, the same sort of thing was explained in connection with sin. Here the redemptive principle works in suffering.

Satan is the "Accuser". It is a good name. Endlessly with unsleeping malice he accuses, nags, labours to convince us ourselves (as well as all creation) that we are weak, damaged, worthless, evil. Well, the Accuser is *"Thrown down"* in the Apocalypse.

3. What God is really like

Sacred Heart

This book is called "Ways of Loving". Love is the purpose of life, the command of God, and indeed his own existence. Since God became man, the absurd title of this section can be filled out: "God is like Jesus; or rather, Jesus *is* true God, and true man; God's character, in our terms, is seen in Jesus on the cross; or if that isn't plain enough — if, as Jesus seems to have said, our own love has grown cold — then it can be summed up in the Heart of God made-man, pierced by man's sin and ablaze with love for him".

Trinity

God is love, we say after St John — to the dismay I suppose of logically minded philosophers. But look at God's nature. God's knowledge is infinite: what is to be "known" in the created universe looks endless to us, but it is not enough — to put it crudely — to exercise infinite wisdom. The only subject "big" enough to hold God's total attention, and beautiful enough and worthy enough, is Himself. God's existence demands that he should, for all eternity, be absorbed and lost in contemplation of Himself. In us, an activity like that would be the most grotesque vanity. But not in God: what else is *worthy* of his attention; what else is big enough or beautiful enough — what else would we *want* him to be doing?

One can picture this knowledge of God as a light streaming from its source and, as it were, crystallising into a mirror — the light held steady enough to be gazed at and loved by the source of the light. This mirror is the Second Person of the Blessed Trinity; the Source is the First. The First is "Father", for he originates. The Second is "Son" for he receives; or "Word", because a word is an uttered thought, and the Second Person is the expression of the Father's thought. The Son, the Word, receives all he is from the Father and, mirror-like, his whole intent and purpose is to reflect back the beauty and light.

The Father expresses Himself totally and perfectly, for he is infinite and the expression of his thought must mirror his life, his self-hood. Thus it is that the Second is a *Person,* because life is given and received. But what would these two Persons do — equally beautiful, "made for each other", endlessly giving, receiving, reflecting — except move together in a great embrace of love? And that love is adequate and worthy of each: the Son properly loves the Father, and the Father the Son: so the love is Itself a Person. Here is the Third. Spirit — a good name, for he is breathed (or whirlwinded?) from each. A ceaseless giving, receiving and returning of self, is what God is "like".

Incarnation

And the Second Person became man. We cannot begin to imagine the human psychology of Jesus, but we should let our minds push as far as they can into "humanity" and "Godhead" if we are to think properly of him. When He speaks about himself, you can see him usually lowering Himself in comparison with the Father — except on rare occasions ("The Father and I are one". "He who sees me sees the Father") when he claims an honour or speaks with an authority or demands a reverence appropriate only to God. As to what it *felt like* to be Jesus, probably these words give the clearest indication — words appropriate to his uncreated Godhead, his work in heaven, as much as to his humanity: "What pleases the Father I ever do". "My meat is to do the will of Him who sent me".

For him to be able to say this, how obvious that there could be no taint of sin. How *could* there be anything in the human heart or heredity or psychology of God-made man which would be unworthy of God? For almost the first time in this book I speak of God's Mother: and say only that *of course* she had to be sinless from the first moment of her conception

57

— for his sake. (How obvious it seems, now that since 1854 we know for certain!). And *of course* her sinless body, which had housed God and passed on to Him everything he needed that was human, *had* to be rejoined to him at the end of her life. And, when it comes to "Ways of Loving", of all the illustrations of what her son did, she is the clearest.

Kenosis

The Incarnation was a real emptying, and Phil 2:6-11 probably tells us more about Jesus, who and what he was and what he did, than any other half-dozen verses in the Bible. But perhaps the most interesting verses, and the ones that give us the best clue as to "why God became man" are Heb 8:9: "Son of God though he was, he learned obedience in the school of suffering, and now, his full achievement reached, he wins eternal salvation for all those who render obedience to him". Who was the "learning" for? Did *he* need a human body, so that suffering and endurance and obedience (that is, love) of a human sort could be presented to the Father in him? How? We suffer, and if we present this to him — "render an obedience to him" — we are able to unite it to his sufferings and obedience and so reach the "full achievement" and "eternal salvation". "What is not assumed (taken on by Jesus) is not redeemed" is a cliché of the Fathers in incarnation controversy. We could put it this way: "*Everything* that is assumed — brought into Christ's humanity — is redeemed". And here is the point of the "healing" described in section 2.

Sinless Redeemer

And sin in Christ? Christ could be assaulted from outside, as it were — by hunger, exhaustion, thirst, injustice as well as by treachery, ingratitude, scourge and nail. And his body and nerves responded humanly. But there was no traitor within him: sin had touched no part of him, and his response was never inadequate and never owed any debt to what was inappropriate. One of the less deplorable catechetical text books for children going the rounds speaks of Jesus being naughty "like other boys . . . " and adult modernists like to speak of Christ experiencing venereal movement. These ideas seem to be, frankly, blasphemous. They are alleged on the grounds that otherwise Christ would not have been truly human. But what seems so human to us, because every man, woman and child we know manifests it, namely weakness, lack of integration, confusion, insensitivity, self-aggrandisement and all the other root evils, are *defects* of humanity. The only *real* human being is Jesus. We are, so to speak, damaged deviations from the norm.

It is vital for us that there should be a *real* human being who is also God. Because he is a real human being, he can experience all our weaknesses. In handling them obediently he receives a "reward" from his Father. This reward is his risen glory as man. Risen as man, and with his power as God, he can share this reward with us — not just in the future but now, as "antidote" to the particular sickness we now experience. That is, *if* we bring it to him. See how the "mystical" and extended body of Christ will enable Christ to pour his saving unction into every wound and every trace of sin — undo (or transform) every moment where Satan's triumphant malice had worked its way.

There could not have been sin, or any result of sin, in Christ. If there had been any least movement of disobedience to God, the Blessed Trinity would have disintegrated. No movement of Christ's human will could ever have disobeyed the divine reason.

4. Union with Christ

He "learned obedience through suffering". The perfection of love (obedience) for Christ was involved with suffering. He would (one thinks) have become man even if there had been no fall and no possibility of suffering, but in a fallen world *de facto* the love and obedience works out through the Cross. That is the high point. And when suffering comes to us, we are then most effectively conformed to Christ as *he* was at his most effective.

Our usefulness to God depends on our degree of union with Christ — on the "sanctifying grace" we have, and on our love. But given that, we would give him greater freedom to work through us if we were literally conformed to him at his clearest instance of loving — namely when we too are crucified.

Suffering rightly handled enables us to be used by God in a special way. Any "suffering": not just martyrdom, or poverty, or obedience; but any "dying" experience. And pre-eminently whatever involves humiliation and death of self. *Even if it is one's own fault,* **if one can turn it to God** and unite it to Christ's passion, that is promotion. The weakness that results in sin: alcoholism, drug addiction, sexual deviation; cowardice, envy, aggression, duplicity, cruelty, meanness; mental weakness, neurosis, depression; pain, cancer, the humiliation of old age and terminal illness . . . if only this is turned to God, and Christ allowed to penetrate where it goes, then *all* is not only well — but immeasurably successful.

It is union with Christ, of course, that is the essential. "Supernatural grace" is a clumsy term, but it means being in-dwelt by Christ, lived in by him, inserted into him, indwelt by the Spirit, being part (because "in Christ") of the love-life of the Blessed Trinity. How much this should mean to us. Some feel that old theology books were obsessed with sin, and when something was "mortal" . . . ridiculous in some aspects, but pardonable. For it is true that *all* that matters is that one should live and die joined to Christ. If I don't die in him, I will never be able to endure the beauty and holiness of God — I'll be stuck with him and find him hateful, without the equipment (Christ's life) that I need. And if I don't now live in him, then Christ cannot use me. I may be living well and generously, but if (unlikely I suppose, but theoretically possible) he does not live in me, my virtuous actions do not extend his penetration of the world.

So how should one think of Christ? Perhaps as straining towards us — nailed indeed to the Cross (that's for our sins, and if he wasn't he would be no use to us) but his eyes are alive with light, love, compassion, eagerness. He strains against the nails in eagerness to embrace. Or, as St Margaret Mary saw him, showing the centre of his humanity ablaze with love for us and given for us. Or as Julian of Norwich *(Revelations of Divine Love, Ch 24)* puts it: "Then with a glad cheer our Lord looked into his side and beheld, rejoicing . . . (and) shewed unto mine understanding, in part, the blessed Godhead . . . And with this our good Lord said full blissfully: 'Lo, how that I loved thee', as if he had said: 'My darling, behold and see thy Lord, thy God that is thy Maker and thine endless joy, see what liking and bliss I have in thy salvation; and for my love enjoy now with me'".

"And also, for more understanding, this blessed word was said: 'Lo, how I loved thee! Behold and see that I loved thee so much ere I died for thee, that I would die for thee; and now I have died for thee and suffered willingly that (which) I may. And now is all my bitter pain and my hard travail turned to endless joy and bliss to me and to thee. How should it now be that thou shouldst anything pray that liketh me, but that I should full gladly grant it thee? For my liking is thy holiness and thine endless joy and bliss with me.'

"This is the understanding, simply as I can say, of this blessed word: 'Lo, how I loved thee'. This showed our good Lord for to make us glad and merry."

Appendix 1:

Family Planning

1. It is almost incredible that in a world with such rapid technological developments, there is so little understanding and appreciation of human fertility and especially of Natural Family Planning (NFP).

Contrary to the belief of many people, the Catholic Church is not against family planning. What have been extensively debated during the past two decades are the forms of family planning that are morally acceptable within a Christian marriage. A great deal of scientific research has gone into Natural Family Planning since the 1950s, and we have progressed a long way from the 'Rhythm' method which for many years was the method mainly used by Catholics.

Natural Family Planning is a means through which a couple may either achieve or avoid a pregnancy. It is based upon a couple's own knowledge of their naturally occurring cyclic phases of fertility and infertility. Natural Family Planning is *not* just another method of contraception, but rather it is true family planning. It provides the couple with the means to be able to express freely their reproductive potential. Besides being a reliable method of avoiding pregnancy it can be used to help achieve a pregnancy, and is particularly helpful for those couples who have difficulty in achieving a pregnancy.

2. Fertility Appreciation

This is the foundation of Natural Family Planning. It is the ability to value, respect and understand our fertility, which is a precious gift from God, and not a disease to be treated by powerful chemicals or surgery. Unfortunately many women value their fertility only when they no longer have it; this highlights the importance of education in the whole area of human sexuality. For this to take place the Church and the state must be prepared to finance schemes to promote high quality training and professional expertise in Natural Family Planning and related topics.

3. Advantages of Natural Family Planning

- It is medically safe, with no adverse side-effects.

- It is highly reliable.

- It is morally acceptable.

- It is easy to learn.

- It costs virtually nothing.

- It can be used at any stage of a woman's reproductive life, e.g. after childbirth, breastfeeding, pre-menopause. It can also be used effectively by women coming off the pill.

- It precisely identifies the true days of fertility and infertility.

In addition to the above advantages, the following make NFP an ideal method of family planning:

- **Shared Responsibility.** Unlike the use of contraceptives, Natural Family Planning methods are equally shared by the man and the woman. Couples learn to understand their combined fertility.

- **A true method of Family Planning.** The same method can be used both to achieve and to avoid pregnancy, making it a genuine method of family planning.

- **Loving Co-operation.** The method helps build a more

loving co-operation in the important matters of sexuality and family planning. It also promotes improved communication in all other areas of their relationship.

- **Enhances one's sexuality.** The couple learns that true sexuality is spiritual, physical, intellectual, creative and emotional in its dimensions. The use of Natural Family Planning assists the couple in developing a balance in their sexual lives. Couples who practice NFP testify to the importance of periodically avoiding genital contact in the growth of their marital relationship.

4. The three main methods of Natural Family Planning

1. Basal Body Temperature (BBT) method.
2. Ovulation method (also known as the Cervical Mucus method or the Billings method).
3. Sympto-Thermal (S-T) method.

Instruction by a qualified teacher of NFP is essential in order to gain confidence in the various methods of Natural Family Planning and to obtain the maximum possible efficiency. The effectiveness of NFP is extremely high when it is properly taught and correctly applied (see below).

5. Effectiveness

There is no method of family planning which is 100% certain; all methods, both artificial (including sterilisation) and natural have a failure rate. The figures shown overleaf represent the probable number of women, out of 100 users, who in a year would conceive a child.

COMPARISON OF FAILURE RATES OF DIFFERENT
METHODS OF BIRTH CONTROL PER 100 WOMAN YEARS

Family Planning Method	Theoretical or method failure	Practical or user failure
Female sterilisation	0.04	0.04
Vasectomy	0.15	0.15
Injectables	0.25	0.25
Combined pill	0.5	2
Mini-pill	1	2.5
IUCD	1.5	4
Condom	2	10
Diaphragm plus spermicide	2	10
Cervical cap	2	13
Spermicide alone	3-5	15
No method of contraception	90	90
NFP: Ovulation method*	0.4	5.2
Sympto-Thermal**	1	2

Source: *Family Planning*, Lawther 1985.
The Ovulation Method of NFP, Dr Thomas W Hilgers, Omaha,
Nebraska, 1983.
**User-effectiveness of Sympto-Thermal Method in Germany*, Petra Frank,
Michael Bremme, Teresa Rosmus, Werner Kunkel, 1987.

There are some points here to ponder in passing. First, even vasectomy and female sterilisation are not "safe"! Secondly, consider the failure rate of the condom — so widely recommended as being "safe" — in the context of Aids. A woman can conceive only 3 or 4 days in the month, yet even with the possibility of conception being *one day in ten*, one in ten women would conceive within one year! How often, therefore, might the HIV virus have passed?

In conclusion, it is reasonable to say that for properly instructed and well-motivated couples, the efficiency of NFP methods compares favourably with the most reliable artificial method, and with no adverse side-effects.

7. Further Information

To obtain further information about NFP contact:

National Association of Natural Family Planning Teachers
Birmingham Maternity Hospital
Queen Elizabeth Medical Centre
Birmingham B15 2TE   **Tel: 021-472 1377**

Natural Family Planning Education Foundation
National Co-ordinators: Brian & Maureen Devine
The Old Rectory
Church Lane
North Ockendon
Essex MR4 3ZH   **Tel: 0709-857122**

Catholic Marriage Advisory Council
Clitherow House
1 Blyth Mews
Blyth Road
London W14 0NW   **Tel: 01-371 1341**

(Based on information provided by John Kelly, FRCS, FRCOG and Sr Nuala O'Connor, SRN, SCM, LNFPP, LNFPE)

Appendix 2:

A healing service

1. Explanation

This service is explained for the sake of priests. It is "non-charismatic". It focuses some of the doctrine in this booklet.

2. Preliminary

Explain the "theory" of healing, presumably at Sunday Mass. Describe the possible "wounds" anyone can receive, and how they may blind us to God's love and prevent us loving and forgiving others.

Tell the people to think and pray through the "wounds". Perhaps to write them down. (Ideally, to talk them through with you — though obviously this would normally not be possible).

Help the people towards forgiveness of those who hurt them.

3. The Service (this follows a few days later):

(a) Expose the Blessed Sacrament.

(b) Help people show the "wounds" to Jesus silently in their hearts.

(c) People come up, one by one, to the priest, who is close to the Blessed Sacrament. They kneel facing it if possible; and perhaps place at the foot of it a short list of deeper wounds which no-one will see.

(d) The priest asks each one:

"Do you believe our Lord can heal every wound you have? . . . "

"Is there any one particular hurt you would like to say now? . . . "

(c) The priest anoints on forehead with blessed oil, saying

"Since Christ died on the Cross
and gave his life to the end,
everything has already been touched
by his saving Passion.
May Christ's touch *(here anoint)*
heal the wounds and bring the Accuser down,
restoring peace in you
and an increase of love."

(f) The priest blesses; concludes:

"Go in the peace of Christ to love and serve the Lord."

(g) Choir, or taped music, with readings interspersed accompany the anointings.

(h) End with Benediction.

Appendix 3

Some Recommended Reading

The following books are not mutually exclusive, but represent a selection which may be helpful:

On Love

Humanae Vitae (CTS)
Familiaris Consortio (CTS)
The Four Loves, C S Lewis (Fontana paperback)

On Chastity

Vatican II, Volumes 1 and 2, Flannery (Fowler Wright) (volume 2 has the key Church's documents subsequent to Vatican II)
. . . And you are Christ's, Fr Thomas Dubay, (Ignatius)
Contraception and Chastity, Dr Elizabeth Anscombe (CTS)

On Natural Family Planning

Fertility Appreciation: The Ovulation method of NFP, Dr Thomas W Hilgers (Creighton University, USA)
The Gift of Life and Love, Dr John J Billings (Apostolate of Catholic Truth, 1987)

On Evil and Suffering

The problem of pain, C S Lewis (Fontana paperback)

On the Mass

The Mass, J-M Lustiger (Collins Fount, 1990)